P-40 WARHAWK
in World War II Color

Jeffrey L. Ethell

Motorbooks International
Publishers & Wholesalers ®

First published in 1994 by Motorbooks International Publishers & Wholesalers, PO Box 2, 729 Prospect Avenue, Osceola, WI 54020 USA

Motorbooks International is a certified trademark, registered with the United States Patent Office

The information in this book is true and complete to the best of our knowledge. All recommendations are made without any guarantee on the part of the author or Publisher, who also disclaim any liability incurred in connection with the use of this data or specific details

We recognize that some words, model names and designations, for example, mentioned herein are the property of the trademark holder. We use them for identification purposes only. This is not an official publication

Motorbooks International books are also available at discounts in bulk quantity for industrial or sales-promotional use. For details write to Special Sales Manager at the Publisher's address

Library of Congress Cataloging-in-Publication Data Available

ISBN 0-87938-928-1

On the front cover: The 15,000th Curtiss fighter was a P-40N painted with the markings of every nation that had flown the company's products. Before the airplane headed off to a line unit, Buffalo factory workers painted over all the insignia. *NASM Arnold Collection*

On the frontispiece: A 36th Squadron, 8th Pursuit Group pilot climbs into the squadron commander's P-40 at Langley. *USAF*

On the title page: An early-production P-40 with no armament runs up before a training flight. These toothless fighters were relegated to training without ever being slated for modification to combat standards. *NASM Groenhoff Collection*

On the back cover: June 1943 brought a major insignia change for American aircraft. Bars were added to the round star and blue background, with a red border surrounding the entire marking. This colorful insignia lasted but a few months before it was replaced. This P-40K out of Randolph Field, Texas, carries the red-bordered star and bars. *USAF via Stan Piet*

Printed and bound in Hong Kong

Contents

Introduction

Hawks

Although the P-40 was deemed obsolete at the time of Japan's attack on Pearl Harbor, for the first year of the Pacific War it was the U.S. Army Air Force's most important fighter, if for no other reason than its availability. Its fame was sealed when Claire Chennault's American Volunteer Group (AVG), the Flying Tigers, successfully fought back the Japanese over China and Burma from December 1941 to July 1942 with their shark-mouthed fighters.

In October 1934, when Curtiss-Wright's Donovan R. Berlin began design work on the Hawk 75—later designated the P-36—he had no idea the airframe, basically unchanged, would live on in over 13,000 Tomahawks, Kittyhawks, and Warhawks (all versions of the P-40). By 1938, the P-36 had become the Army Air Corps' primary fighter, and Berlin got the Army's blessing to modify it by hanging an Allison V-1710 up front in place of the usual Pratt & Whitney R-1830. The result was the turbo-supercharged XP-37 which yielded 340 miles per hour at 20,000 feet—when the turbo worked. By December 1937 another thirteen YP-37s were ordered by the Army Air Corps

in hopes that the turbo's problems could be ironed out. Unfortunately, that was not to be.

Berlin tried a different tack. In standard trim, the 1710 made 1,090 horsepower at 10,000 feet. To up the power, Berlin asked Allison to step up the rpm of the 1710's single-stage mechanical supercharger. This V-1710-19 was installed in the tenth production P-36 airframe—modified with a belly scoop radiator—and flown for the first time on 14 October 1938. Dubbed the XP-40, it won the Army Air Corps' May 1939 fighter competition at Wright Field with a top speed of 365 miles per hour at 15,000 feet. The Army immediately ordered 524 examples. The $13 million tab was the largest fighter contract in American history.

In one of a number of top-level decisions indicative of what would later spell doom for the company, Curtiss-Wright management ordered Berlin to redesign the aircraft to mount the radiator under the nose. They thought it looked better this way, though it cost the aircraft speed. On 4 April 1940 test pilot Lloyd Childs flew the first production P-40, and by 1 June the Army began to take delivery of an aircraft that, from the firewall back, was essentially unchanged from its introduction in 1934. In September, the 8th Pursuit Group at Langley Field, Virginia, became the first AAC unit to convert to P-40s. The 20th Group at March Field, California, and the 31st Group at Selfridge Field, Michigan, soon followed suit.

Berlin was well aware of the aircraft's limitations. As the first P-40Bs were rolling off the Buffalo factory assembly lines in May 1941, Berlin was in England to question RAF pilots about the relative merits of British and German aircraft. After a glimpse of Rolls-Royce testing its new Merlin 60 engine, he quickly asked for this two-speed, two-stage supercharged, high-altitude engine for the P-40. Unfortunately, he was only able to swing the low-altitude Merlin 28 (for the P-40F and L), just slightly better than the 1,150-horsepower V-1710-39 being installed in P-40Es at the end of 1941. As a result, the P-40 was forever destined to be a low-altitude fighter. Berlin was so frustrated by Curtiss' lack of management and engineering foresight that he resigned at the end of December 1941, when only about 1,000 P-40s had been built, and went to work for General Motors.

Tomahawks

The first fifty-five Army Air Corps P-40Bs went overseas with the 15th and 18th Pursuit Groups at Wheeler Field, Hawaii. Another thirty-one went to the 20th Squadron, 24th Pursuit Group in the Philippines. The 33rd Pursuit Squadron was detached from the 8th Group to fly their P-40s to Iceland on 25 July 1941. The 35th Pursuit Squadron, 36th Group had gone to Puerto Rico the previous April, and the 16th Group had gone to Panama.

Through the P-40C, which first flew on 10 April 1941, all Hawk 81s (as the company called them) looked the same. A substantial number of these went to Britain's RAF as the Tomahawk Mk.I and II. By this time the Curtiss plant was running at maximum capacity with thirty production test pilots running from one P-40 to the next. To save time, new fighters were often flown out of the parking lot next to the plant instead of being trucked to the Buffalo Airport. The parking lot/landing strip was only 1,100 feet long and just slightly wider than a P-40's wingspan.

When the Japanese attacked Pearl Harbor on 7 December 1941 most of the P-36s and P-40s were lined up at Wheeler and Bellows Fields with empty fuel tanks and no ammunition, and the majority of them were destroyed in short order. Fortunately, almost unnoticed by the Japanese, the 47th Squadron had eight P-40Bs and six P-36As detached to the dirt strip at Haleiwa for gunnery training. Three 44th Squadron P-40Cs got airborne in the middle of the attack at Bellows, but all were shot down. Five pilots managed to get up to Haleiwa, under attack by a Val, and get two P-40s and five P-36s into the air. Though several kills were claimed against Japanese aircraft, by the end of the day there were only two P-40Cs, twenty-five P-40Bs, and sixteen P-36s still airworthy.

In the Philippines, the 24th Pursuit Group lost twenty-six P-40s, including some new E models, as well as the majority of its P-35s and obsolete P-26s. Most were hit on the ground at Clark and Iba Fields, though some pilots did get into the air; others were shot down on take-off.

In May 1941, the first RAF Tomahawks went into combat with No.250 Squadron in the Middle

East, followed by No.3 Squadron RAAF (Royal Australian Air Force), and No.2 Squadron SAAF (South African Air Force). By November, No.112 SquadronRAF and No.4 Squadron SAAF were flying Tomahawk IIBs over the Western Desert. Pilots were generally delighted with the rugged nature and excellent hitting power of the small fighter, finding few areas to complain about. Most aerial combat in the desert took place below 10,000 feet, making the Tomahawk an excellent dogfighter as well as a hard-hitting, close-air-support attack aircraft.

When the Flying Tigers took their 100 diverted ex-RAF Hawk 81A-2s (Tomahawk IIs) into combat in December 1941, they confirmed the British impression that the P-40 was an exceptional low-level fighter. Though they could not turn quite as tight as their opponents, mostly Ki.43 Hayabusas (even more maneuverable than the vaunted Zero), the Tigers found their Hawks could take on the opposition and win. High diving speed, rugged construction, armor protection, good firepower, and light controls made an excellent combination that enabled them to stop the Japanese in the air at a time when few others were able to do so. The Flying Tigers' signature shark mouths were copied straight off those painted on RAF No.112 Squadron's desert Tomahawks.

Kittyhawks

With the P-40D, the H87, came a major redesign including an enlarged radiator and oil cooler scoop, a new canopy, a fuselage shortened by six inches, shorter landing gear, removal of the fuselage guns, the addition of four .50 caliber guns in the wings, and a higher propeller thrust line.

When the P-40E flew for the first time in mid-1941 it had six .50s in the wings—standard armament from that point on. All subsequent P-40s stayed with the H87 designator; the British called them Kittyhawks, and the Army Air Forces eventually renamed its P-40s Warhawks.

Fortunately for the Army, there were enough P-40s on hand to keep throwing them into the breech against the seemingly unstoppable Japanese. The version most responsible for holding the fort in those dark days was the P-40E, built in larger numbers (2,320) than any other Hawk except the P-40N. Unfortunately, the E was more prone than previous models to swinging left on take-off, a problem wrestled with for some time. In a dive the controls got stiff while the aircraft tended to skid severely to the right even with full left rudder. The extended fuselages of later models solved these problems to a large degree.

Against overwhelming odds, Army pilots in the Philippines fought on. Most of the remaining P-40s were merged into a single Flying Detachment. Twenty Army pilots and their ground crews moved to Bataan Field with seven P-40Es and two P-40Bs and flew strafing, bombing, and recce missions from mid-January to early-April 1942. Though these brave men managed to get twelve kills and hold the Japanese invaders at bay to some degree, finally there was but a single P-40 left, this one assembled from the parts of the remaining aircraft. The day Bataan fell, the lone P-40E was flown out to northern Mindanao where four other P-40Es were still flying combat. When the islands were finally surrendered on 6 May 1942, the remnants of the Battling Bastards of Bataan's air force were blown up by the Americans.

Warhawks

The decimated 24th Pursuit (soon redesignated Fighter along with all other AAF fighter units) Group was reformed in Australia (with detachments sent to Java) in early 1942. The 24th was supplemented by the 49th Fighter Group which successfully defended northern Australia out of Darwin by shooting down numerous Japanese bombers and fighters. The 49th transferred to Port Moresby, New Guinea, in mid-1942 and flew Warhawks right up through the N model in 1943 before switching to P-38s. Another chopped-up unit, the 18th Fighter Group, got new P-40s and flew combat out of Guadalcanal with the E, F, M, and N models. In the Central Pacific, the mauled 15th Fighter Group flew an island-hopping campaign with a succession of models through the N until re-equipped with P-51s in 1944.

When the Flying Tigers were disbanded on 4 July 1942, the remnants became the China-based 23rd Fighter Group. The P-40E-equipped 51st Fighter Group formed in India, and by June 1943 two squadrons of the 80th Fighter Group were flying skull-nosed Warhawks out of Upper Assam, India. From their base in the Aleutians, the 11th and 18th Fighter Squadrons began fighting the Japanese in June 1942, while in the Mediterranean the 57th Fighter Group flew their first missions out of Palestine in August with P-40Fs and Ks.

Although the P-40F was powered by the Merlin 28, the Allison line kept going with the P-40K, which, like the F (after 699 were built), had 20 inches added to the fuselage midway through the production run to counter tail buffet. (As it turned out, the problem was an improperly redesigned scoop for the Merlin, something which fell on deaf ears despite Donovan Berlin's pleadings—yet another reason he left Curtiss-Wright.) Although at 10,000 pounds the K had the highest gross weight of any P-40 (the XP-40 weighed in at 6,870 pounds), the added horsepower of the modified Allison boosted top speed to 360 miles per hour.

During Operation Torch, the 8 November 1942 invasion of North Africa, the 33rd Fighter Group flew its P-40Fs off the carrier *Chenango* to Morocco while the 79th Group was delivered to Egypt by the *Ranger*. The 324th Fighter Group brought its Warhawks to the theater in December. The highlight of American P-40 operations in the Mediterranean took place on 18 April 1943, during the Palm Sunday Massacre. A formation of forty-seven Warhawks from the 57th and 324th Groups, covered by twelve RAF Spitfires, intercepted a mass formation of Ju 52s resupplying Rommel. In a short time fifty-eight Junkers transports were claimed destroyed along with eighteen Macchi 202 and Messerschmitt 109 escort fighters for the loss of one Spitfire and four P-40s.

April also saw both the P-40F-outfitted 325th Fighter Group and the all-black 99th Fighter Squadron (flying Warhawks handed down from other groups) enter combat from Africa. The 99th, in concert with three more squadrons, became the segregated 332nd Fighter Group. Both the 325th and the 332nd groups would later take their P-40s to Italy before re-equipping with P-47s.

The stripped-down "Gypsy Rose Lee" version of the Merlin-powered F was the L with four wing guns, less armor, lower fuel capacity, and some other things removed, to save about 250 pounds. A shortage of Merlin parts resulted in 300 Fs and Ls being re-engined with Allisons then relegated to training command as P-40Rs.

Out of the L and its Allison-powered M brother came the most-produced Warhawk, the P-40N, a direct approach to increasing performance by reducing gross weight to 8,850 pounds. With a 1,200-horsepower V-1710-81, the N squeaked to 378 miles per hour, which by 1943 standards was well below other first-line types.

In spite of its lesser performance, the P-40 continued to be used right up to the end of the war by such diverse combat units as the AAF and RAF Commonwealth forces of Australia, Canada, South Africa, and New Zealand, as well as the air forces of Russia, China, and France. The last P-40 of 13,737 built, a P-40N-40-CU (44-47964), rolled off the line on 30 November 1944. To give an idea of what mass production could do, the P-40B cost $60,562 in 1941 while the P-40N of 1944 cost $44,892. The homefront American industrial worker performed a production miracle that won World War II.

The last version, the XP-40Q, had a bubble canopy and a four-bladed propeller. Created from a P-40K-1, it was far too late, arriving at Wright Field in early 1945 for evaluation. With a high-altitude Allison V-1710-121 producing 1,425 horsepower, it finally got up there with the big boys,

able to top out at 422 miles per hour with a service ceiling of 39,000 feet.

Universally, P-40 pilots loved their airplane, many choosing to continue flying it even when other more powerful types were offered. Bill Stubbs, who flew in the Mediterranean, confirmed that "the P-40 could outdive about anything, and indicated airspeeds of 600 miles per hour were not unheard of. However, it did want to pull to the right in a dive, and when it was desirable to hold it straight, as for dive bombing, it needed a lot of left rudder pressure—so much so that it was alleged that one could always spot a P-40 pilot by the over-developed muscles in his left leg."

R. T. Smith, one of the AVG's aces, thought the Curtiss fighter served the Flying Tigers well. "I really loved that old P-40. It was reliable, could take a helluva beating and still get back home, and if you pointed the damn thing in the right direction you could get pretty good results. I was mad as hell when another guy cracked up my old No. 77 while I was on a ferry trip to Africa. It gets to be quite a personal feeling for your own airplane, the one with your name painted up near the cockpit, and none of the others ever feel quite the same. Sorta like members of the opposite sex, maybe: they're all built more or less identical, but . . . "

P–40 Warhawk Photo Gallery

The family resemblance between this Wright Field Materiel Division Curtiss P-36 and the P-40 is unmistakable. The tenth production P-36 became the XP-40 with the only major change being an Allison V-1710 in place of the Pratt & Whitney R-1830. The result was near instant obsolescence when compared to the fighters being built in Europe and Japan. *NASM Arnold Collection via Stan Piet*

Previous page
New P-36Cs of the 36th Pursuit Group on the line at Langley Field, Virginia. The P-36 was a wonderful aircraft to fly according to its pilots—a real sports car with light controls and excellent maneuverability. Unfortunately its top speed of 323 miles per hour (the P-36A only managed 300 miles per hour) was far below modern standards, a reflection on the state of an American aircraft industry struggling through the Depression and isolationism. *USAF via Stan Piet*

Above
These 27th Squadron, 1st Pursuit Group P-36Cs sit ready for the National Air Races, September 1939. The garish camouflage was created specifically to make an Army splash at the races, and it was never used in the maneuvers or wargames for which such schemes were normally slated. The 27th Squadron badge is just visible behind the wingtip of No.69. No two of the schemes were alike. *USAF*

14

In early 1941, the aspirations for modern fighters in the
U.S. Army Air Corps were pinned on these four
aircraft. From top to bottom are the second YP-38
Lightning, a production Bell P-39C Airacobra, a
production P-40, and a Republic YP-43 Lancer. The P-
38 was the best of the lot. The lengthened tailwheel strut
on the P-40 is fixed down as a stopgap measure to
improve the fighter's ground looping characteristics.
NASM Arnold Collection

Next page
The XP-40 in its final form (the radiator was moved
from the belly to the front, much to designer Don
Berlin's disgust) without armor or armament was
assigned to the Air Corps Materiel Division, Wright
Field, Ohio. The stripped "hot rod" prototype had
excellent performance when compared to heavier
service models. *NASM Arnold Collection*

A 33rd Squadron, 8th Pursuit Group P-40 at Langley Field, Virginia, 1941, just after the group became the first in the Air Corps to be equipped with the type. It was standard practice to paint the squadron emblem on the side of each fighter, adding some much-needed color to an otherwise drab aircraft. Other flights in the squadron had yellow and white nose markings. *USAF via Stan Piet*

Next page
Time for a flight marking change as the mechanic oversprays what used to be a red nosed (and before that blue) Tomahawk. Markings were never pristine when viewed up close—there was a job to be done and ground crew did not have a great deal of time to make things look perfect. The chamois-padded, rubber ear headset was typical equipment for the day, resulting in extensive hearing loss. The rubber never seemed to enclose the ears as much as smash them flat. The headsets were good, however, for producing that fifty mission crush look on one's hat. *USAF*

A 35th Squadron, 8th Pursuit Group pilot climbs from P-40-CU serial number 39-189 at Mitchel Field, Long Island. It wouldn't take long to go deaf wearing only this regulation Army issue headset, and the A-2 jacket provided absolutely no warmth, being good for little more than show. The first production P-40s did not have letter suffix model designations, something that didn't come along until the P-40B; this was the case on all other Army aircraft as well. Lack of model designations led to a fair amount of confusion, so the system was later changed to give the first production runs of new aircraft an "A model" suffix. *NASM Arnold Collection via Stan Piet*

Mechanics hover around an early P-40-CU at Mitchel Field. The fighter's tightly cowled engine proved to be a knuckle-busting nightmare, particularly in the harsh conditions of combat. The closer the cowling, the higher the speed, but when a mechanic had to shove his bare hands up into a blistering hot engine compartment, he wasn't that impressed by airspeed. Can you imagine doing this with two Allisons on the same aircraft? The number of men here is about right—it took a ground crew long hours of work each day to keep a World War II fighter airworthy. *NASM Arnold Collection via Stan Piet*

Previous page
Standard 1941 high-altitude flying equipment is
modeled by this 8th Pursuit Group pilot at Mitchel
Field. The bladder oxygen mask would later give way
to diluter-demand systems, but the helmet, goggles, and
shearling leather suit and boots would remain standard,
particularly for bomber crews, through most of the war
until replaced by electrically heated garments. These
suits were particularly bulky in the tight confines of a
fighter cockpit and many pilots elected to wear multiple
layers of long underwear and wool clothing instead.
The last thing a pilot wanted in combat was the
inability to move quickly from side to side and look
directly to the rear. *NASM Arnold Collection via
Stan Piet*

A flight of unarmed early-production P-40-CUs climbs
out on a training flight in late-1940. Each of the Hawk
pilots has opened the radiator gills under the rear
section of the nose to get increased cooling of the
Prestone glycol/water mixture. From the P-40's first
days, overheating was a constant problem, particularly
when taxiing. Much of the problem had to do with the
radiator subcontractors, as some manufacturers built
units that seemed to have no problem at all, while
others built radiators that caused the coolant to boil
over. Curtiss pilots watched their engine temperature
gauges more than any other single thing in the cockpit.
NASM Groenhoff Collection

Army pilots do a little staged preflight planning for the photographer with their new P-40Cs in the summer of 1941. Just visible on the wing leading edges are the cutouts for two .30 caliber guns per side—standard armament, along with the nose-mounted .50s, for the C. The B had only one .30 caliber gun per wing, while the P-40 (no letter suffix), had only the nose-mounted .50s. From a distance the differences in these early Hawk 81s are hard to distinguish, a problem compounded when a full complement of guns was not installed. *NASM Groenhoff Collection*

The calm before the storm. A 20th Pursuit Squadron P-40B cruises over Clark Field, Philippines, in the summer of 1941. Ill-prepared for war, the Army Air Forces had a hard time fielding modern equipment, let alone enough of it. Knowing what would happen if war started, 20th Squadron pilot Max Louk wrote home in November that they were "doomed at the start." There would never be another summer quite as idyllic as that year in the Philippines, a Pacific paradise for the prewar Army. *Fred Roberts via William H. Bartsch*

The AVG line at Kunming, early 1942, shows the Fleet Finch trainer used as a hack by the pilots and the fine dirt area which caused constant trouble with the Allison engines. By May the Hawks were so worn out that only small formations could be put up at any one time. The more success Chennault's boys had, the more difficult it seemed to be to get U.S. Army support, particularly in the form of replacement aircraft. During their entire time in combat, the Flying Tigers received a total of thirty P-40Es which Chennault had to sweet-talk the AAF powers-that-be into letting him divert from their original destination (Java). *R. T. Smith*

American Volunteer Group ace R. T. Smith sits in the cockpit of Hawk 81A-2 No.40 at Kunming, China, in early 1942. Claire Chennault's Flying Tigers made the P-40 famous by giving the Japanese a real trouncing in the first six months of the war. Basically export versions of the P-40C, the AVG's diverted RAF Tomahawk IIs were emblazoned with Walt Disney's flying tiger decal, which had been created and shipped to Chennault free of charge. For preservation, each of the decals was shellacked, clearly evident on No.40. *R. T. Smith*

Hell's Angels, Third Squadron, Flying Tigers on patrol over the Burma/China border, mid-morning, 28 May 1942. In the lead is Hell's Angels Squadron Leader Arvid "Oley" Olson flying Chuck Older's No.68 as the six fighters (including R. T. Smith's No.77 from which this shot was taken) head northeast near the Salween River toward Pao Shan to intercept a possible Japanese bombing raid. In echelon behind Olson are Bill Reed, Tom Haywood, Bob Prescott, and Ken Jernstedt. After about an hour with no enemy contact they headed back to Yunnanyi to refuel, then home to Kunming. *R. T. Smith*

This P-40-CU serial number 39-184 was flown out of Luke Field, Arizona, for fighter transition training. As with all the other early "plain vanilla" P-40s they lacked self-sealing fuel tanks, armor, and guns making them light and fun to fly, though they did get long in the tooth by 1942 when this photo was taken. In late 1941, when the author's father, Erv Ethell, was flying one of these P-40s at Luke during the last part of Advanced Flight Training, he heard a tremendous banging as he was cruising along. Sure the fighter was coming apart in the air, he slid the canopy back, unstrapped and started to climb out on the wing to jump when he noticed the sandpaper-type wingwalk had come unglued and was flapping madly against the metal skin. He sheepishly got back in and turned for Luke. *USAF via Stan Piet*

Previous page
The two aircraft types used for Advanced Flight Training at Luke Field in 1941 and 1942—a P-40-CU and an AT-6C—cruise over the Arizona desert. A select number of promising Advanced students were selected from their class to fly the last ten hours of their training in the P-40, which usually meant they were assured of getting fighters upon receiving their wings. Moving from the Texan to the Hawk was breathtaking, the fulfillment of a dream to be an Army fighter pilot. *USAF via Stan Piet*

This new P-40D over Buffalo represents the first major reconfiguration in the fighter's shape. The company changed its internal designation from Hawk 81 to Hawk 87. Though the British changed their name for the P-40 from Tomahawk to Kittyhawk with this version, the latter did not really take with U.S. Army versions, which were called, for the most part, Warhawks from this point on. The new Allison engine had an external reduction gear (earlier versions had used an internal reduction gear) which made the powerplant shorter and resulted in a raised thrust line, which in turn allowed the landing gear to be shortened. The radiator was enlarged and moved farther forward, and the guns in the nose were removed. *NASM Arnold Collection*

When the P-40E came along it was smack in the middle of the strong British buy of Kittyhawks. This Kittyhawk IA had some stars slapped on it and was sold to the Air Corps as a P-40E complete with its standard RAF paint scheme, which was labeled medium green and sand with light blue undersurfaces. In the middle of the E production run Pearl Harbor was attacked and this model became the Army fighter that held the fort for the first year of war. *NASM Groenhoff Collection*

Next page
Three of Curtiss-Wright's most experienced test pilots, Byron Glover, C-W Chief Test Pilot H. Lloyd Childs, and Russell Thaw, with a new Merlin-powered P-40F at the Kenmore Plant in Buffalo. These men are wearing the adapted hard car racing helmets common with many company test pilots across the country—a trend that would eventually lead to hard aviation helmets becoming standard. The Merlin-engined P-40s were easy to recognize as they had no carburetor air scoop atop the cowling. At its height, Curtiss-Wright at Buffalo kept thirty production test pilots on the run to keep the flow of aircraft unhindered. *NASM Arnold Collection via Stan Piet*

A 343rd Fighter Group Warhawk taxies off the runway at Longview Field, Adak, Aleutian Islands, in late 1942. Blowing snow was far preferable to ice or mud, though anything but dry conditions could cause a pilot to lose control of his aircraft. As it was, the P-40 was a ground looper—it didn't need any help. The P-38s on the line across the field belong to the 54th Fighter Squadron, the first unit to take the Lightning fighter into combat the previous September. *National Archives*

Combat duty in the Aleutian Islands was only slightly better than miserable, even on a good day—which meant a day when it wasn't snowing, sleeting, or covering everything with a sheet of ice. This 343rd Fighter Group flight line at Adak on 9 April 1943 gives a good idea of what it was like. The ice and snow has been cleared off the pierced steel plank (PSP) where aircraft have to move or park, and the fuel truck is the mighty Cletrac, which could move through just about anything, whether mud, snow, or ice. The men and women of the 11th Air Force in the Aleutians were all but forgotten as the rest of the war seemed to overshadow them. *National Archives*

Bengal Tigers of the 11th Fighter Squadron parked at Adak, Aleutian Islands in mid-1943. Commanded by Col. John "Jack" Chennault, son of Gen. Claire Chennault, the 11th's P-40s were painted in a variation on the theme made so famous by the Flying Tigers. Pierced steel plank was an absolute necessity for operations in Alaska...otherwise the aircraft would have bogged down in the constant mud. *National Archives*

A Cletrac tows an 11th Fighter Squadron Bengal Tiger Warhawk down the 28th Composite Group line at Adak in the spring of 1943. The lower cowling has been replaced and the tiger face has yet to be repainted, though a squadron emblem remains. Fighter cockpits were notoriously cold with seemingly little thought given to ducting some of the Allison's great heat back to the pilot. In the Aleutians it was even worse because pilots started out cold from long nights in ill-equipped tents. Getting warm was a major pastime. *Via David W. Menard*

One of the maintenance areas at Adak, late 1942— rarely was anything done inside. The 28th Composite Group had a wide variety of aircraft under its wing since there were rarely enough squadrons of a single type to create a specialized outfit. As a result, mechanics had to work on fighters, bombers, and liaison types interchangeably. At least the Allison engine was common to the P-38, -39, and -40. From he looks of the propellers on the Warhawks to the left, the first was probably bellied in while the second had a prop strike, probably from nosing over enough to tip the prop. *National Archives*

P-40Fs of the 33rd Fighter Group are officially presented to the French GC II/5 Groupe Lafayette, or Lafayette Escradrille, at Casablanca, 9 January 1943. Though the 33rd could not afford to lose any of its Warhawks, Allied planners believed it important to re-equip this French unit quickly since it had been a Vichy unit fighting against the Allies during the invasion of North Africa. As soon as the French took delivery of twenty-five P-40Fs on 25 November 1942, two weeks after the invasion, two of the pilots defected to German-occupied southern France with their new Hawk fighters. Nevertheless, the group fought with the Allies, eventually re-equipping with P-40Ls, then P-47Ds. *USAF*

Yessir, living in the Aleutians was sure great fun. Though all theaters of war had problems with mud, when it was frozen it seemed to be about as bad as it could get. The Jeeps and the Dodge Command Car here were about the only method of transportation, aside from the Cletrac, that could manage the muck, but even these were often left sitting in favor of walking. Flying airplanes was the least of one's worries. *National Archives*

The famous World War I Sioux Indian head, Lafayette Escadrille, insignia adorns the side of this Free French GC II/5 P-40F at Casablanca on 9 January 1943. The French Armee de l'Air Catholic priest, who also wears a pilot's brevet and decorations, had blessed the aircraft before taking time to talk to these AAF pilots. The Groupe, which had flown Hawk 75A-4s against the Allies as a Vichy unit, went on to fight with distinction in the Tunisian campaign, once again flying the flag of the famous American pilots who had fought so well as volunteers twenty-five years earlier. *USAF via Stan Piet*

Charles "Jazz" Jaslow with Phil Cochran's 57th Fighter Group P-40E at Bradley Field, Connecticut, in May 1942 just before the unit shipped out for Palestine. Cochran would later become famous for his combat flying in the China-Burma-India Theater as head of the 1st Air Commando Group. Cartoonist Milton Caniff had much to do with this by creating his thinly veiled "Terry and the Pirates" character Flip Corkin. The Group, along with all other AAF fighter units, had been redesignated from "pursuit" to "fighter" on 15 May 1942. *Charles Jaslow*

Though squadron emblems were normal decoration on Army fighters through 1942, the practice, on the whole, was dropped by almost all units except the 57th Fighter Group, which carried the decorations through their combat days in the P-40 and P-47, then into the postwar era with jets. Jazz Jaslow leans on the 65th Squadron CO's P-40E at Bradley Field, Connecticut, May 1942. The 56th's fighting gamecock, with the chip of wood on his right shoulder, made a great piece of art. *Charles Jaslow*

These pilots of B Flight, 87th Squadron, 79th Fighter Group at Rentschler Field, Connecticut, were transferred intact from the 65th Squadron, 57th Fighter Group when the 57th was moved overseas in early July 1942. Around the 87th Squadron "Skeeters" emblem are Scotty Rogers, Frank Huff, James Hundley, Leo Berinati, Ed Holston, John Dzamba, Charles Jaslow, and Red Crossley. By November these men would be in combat in Egypt. *Charles Jaslow*

Lt. Jazz Jaslow (right) with his crew chief R. Randall and their 87th Squadron, 79th Fighter Group P-40F X81 *Sweet Bets*. Jaslow drew Dopey on the rudder using crayons, the only medium he could find, along with the phrase "Passionate Dwarf." Jaslow picked the Disney character because he was considered the small fry of the squadron. Rudder art was common on North African Warhawks. *Charles Jaslow*

Jazz Jaslow with the other end of his 87th Fighter Squadron P-40F *Sweet Bets*, which featured an enlarged version (compared to the previous stateside shot) of the "Skeeters" squadron insignia on the nose. The telltale lack of a carburetor air scoop atop the cowling was an easy way to spot all Merlin-engined P-40s, including the Ls. The RAF Sand and Stone/Azure Blue camouflage was an improvement over solid AAF Olive Drab and Gray in the barren wastes of the Western Desert. *Charles Jaslow*

Pilots and Warhawks, 87th Fighter Squadron, 79th Fighter Group, ready to "crank" at Castel Benito Airdrome, Tripoli, Libya, March 1943. The constant dust/mud of North Africa was rough on both planes and pilots—it seemed to be in the food, the oil, the bedding, the eyes, everything. The only respite was to get airborne. Sitting alert in the hot sun was close to insanity at times. *Charles Jaslow*

The 87th Fighter Squadron spread out across the field at Houaria Landing Ground at the tip of Cape Bon, Tunisia, in the spring of 1943. This bit of Africa which stuck out into the Mediterranean was a good spot for the P-40s. Any Luftwaffe incursions from Sicily and Italy could be intercepted rapidly, particularly the formations of lumbering, near defenseless Ju 52s carrying troops and supplies to Rommel. *Charles Jaslow*

The Me 109 kill on Jazz Jaslow's P-40F reflect the results of a successful fight on 2 April 1943 near Wadi Akarit. From a certain point in the F model's production run forward, with the exception of the K and some other later airframes, Curtiss fitted an ice window to the left front windshield. No one ever seemed to know why, since very few P-40 pilots fought under conditions where ice would be a problem; besides, the canopy could be opened in flight at all speeds. All the ice window really seemed to do was further reduce the already restricted visibility. *Charles Jaslow*

Out to see the sights, 87th Fighter Squadron pilots.
Charles Jaslow

This German Kübelwagen, the enemy's Volkswagen-built version of the Jeep, was requisitioned in good working order by Jazz Jaslow in the desert so he could learn to drive! The 87th Fighter Squadron combat pilot was flying Warhawks but had never been taught the intricacies of the automobile. By the time the squadron moved on he had learned, thanks to the Germans. *Charles Jaslow*

The remains of Scotty Rogers' P-40F after the 87th Squadron's first night landing in the desert. Unable to see, he taxiied into a 55-gallon gas drum which promptly blew up. So much for one relatively new Warhawk. Fortunately the pilot walked away. *Charles Jaslow*

Pilot Jazz Jaslow and his 87th Fighter Squadron crew chief, R. Randall, on Jaslow's P-40F, *Sweet Bets,* spring 1943, proudly frame Jaslow's 2 April 1943 Me 109 kill. The 87th, a part of the 79th Fighter Group, was in Egypt by November 1942, then fought through Libya, Tunisia, Malta, Sicily, and Italy, in addition to a short spell in southern France. Before it was all over, the squadron received two Distinguished Unit Citations, one for combat over North Africa and Sicily from March through August 1943 and the other for action over Italy 16–20 April 1945. *Charles Jaslow*

Spread across the field at Asmara, Eritrea, are new P-40s, ready for test flying over the Abyssinian mountains before heading off to combat. The woodie station wagon, a real find in this barren wasteland, had been commandeered by the Army for use on the field. Some of the 79th Fighter Group's pilots had to fly down to this field to pick up spare aircraft that had been shipped over in crates on freighters, hauled up to the mountains 7,000 feet above sea level, assembled , test flown, and then delivered to the fighter squadrons in the field. *Charles Jaslow*

A 33rd Fighter Group P-40E sits ready at Martin Field, Baltimore, Maryland, in early 1942 as the unit works up for combat. The markings below the wings still include the red-centered star and U.S. ARMY. Both were eliminated in short order, the former because of confusion between it and the Japanese Hinomaru rising sun. By the end of the year, the 33rd would be in combat over North Africa. *J. P. Crowder via Dorothy Helen Crowder*

June 1942: A 33rd Fighter Group P-40F Warhawk over Maryland during lead-in combat training. The red-centered stars are gone, as is the large lettering under the wings. This is the Merlin-engined model the group would also take into combat over the desert, a fortunate happenstance which was often not the case. Many groups would train in one type, then end up with an entirely different aircraft in the combat zone.
J. P. Crowder via Dorothy Helen Crowder

A 33rd Fighter Group P-40F on the Harrisburg, Pennsylvania, ramp of the 103rd Observation Squadron, National Guard. A brand new PT-19, on a test flight from the Fairchild factory at Hagerstown, Maryland, shares the space. The Douglas O-46A was based at the field with the 103rd. Before heading overseas, fighter pilots enjoyed the best of times with the ability to take their aircraft just about anywhere to visit family or buzz everything in sight. It was the world's best flying club, but that would change in a heartbeat once overseas. *J. P. Crowder via Dorothy Helen Crowder*

Next page
A steel helmet was standard issue for fighter pilots in North Africa since they lived out in the open, in tents or foxholes. John P. "Jeep" Crowder stands in front of his 59th Squadron, 33rd Fighter Group P-40F at Thelepte, Tunisia, early-1943. *J. P. Crowder via Dorothy Helen Crowder*

Sunset at Thelepte in the Tunisian desert, January 1943. North Africa was a torture chamber of temperature changes—hot and windy in the daytime, freezing and pitch black at night. Getting warm seemed an impossible task with the standard-issue Army blankets and tents. Some crews preferred to sleep in their aircraft, a real task in a fighter. *J. P. Crowder via Dorothy Helen Crowder*

The sum total of 59th Fighter Squadron operations at Thelepte, Tunisia, January 1943—nothing more, nothing less than a hole in the ground. Though the ground was baked hard, seemingly impervious to the Army issue spade, it was worth the effort to get out of the wind. Additionally, the holes provided air raid protection from anything but a direct hit. *J. P. Crowder via Dorothy Helen Crowder*

An extended fuselage P-40L Warhawk of the 59th Squadron, 33rd Fighter Group, cruises over North Africa, early-1943. The group had flown its fighters off the aircraft carrier USS *Chenango* as a part of Operation Torch the previous November, then set up bare-base operations in French Morocco. The large American flag painted on the side was one of many attempts to identify American planes to the Vichy French defenders, implying the invasion was an all-American operation. The French had little love for the British so the Allied strategy was to play down British participation. *J. P. Crowder via Dorothy Helen Crowder*

The 324th Fighter Group gave up its Warhawks for Thunderbolts. By then its P-40Ls, such as this 316th Squadron aircraft at Foggia Main were well worn. The fighter has a fair amount of fresh olive drab paint over past markings, indicating it had served several pilots and squadrons. The Merlin-powered P-40L was a lightweight, extended fuselage (starting with the L-5) version of the F with only four guns, so it was something of a hot rod even at combat weights. *Fred E. Bamberger, Jr.*

Ben Duke and his crew chief sit alert at the 8th Pursuit Squadron, 49th Pursuit Group revetment at Strauss Airstrip, 27 miles outside Darwin, Australia, in early May 1942. The P-40E is covered with camouflage netting, a very real necessity since northern Australia was under constant Japanese attack. *Clyde H. Barnett, Jr.*

Clyde Barnett's 8th Squadron, 49th Fighter Group
P-40E sits opposite the alert hut under camouflage
netting at Strauss Airstrip outside Darwin, Australia,
May 1942. Barnett recorded in his diary one day, "I am
sitting in the alert hut at the south end of the strip, on
the 5-minute alert, with Blue Flight. Red Flight is on
15-minute today so get to stay at the mess until
needed." *Clyde H. Barnett, Jr.*

Since he was a West Palm Beach native, Clyde Barnett
painted the appropriate nose art on his 8th Squadron,
49th Fighter Group P-40E. This photo was taken at
Kila Kila, New Guinea, in late 1942. Barnett got four
kills in P-40s—two Betty bombers in April 1942, then
two more Japanese aircraft in 1943—before going
home. *Clyde H. Barnett, Jr.*

Continuing to paint his Warhawk, Clyde Barnett included a scene from West Palm Beach and Donald Duck jabbering from behind the star. The 49th Fighter Group had some particularly colorful P-40s with art appearing at several locations on the aircraft. *Clyde H. Barnett, Jr.*

Next page
Blue Flight, 8th Squadron, 49th Pursuit Group on patrol over Darwin in late- April 1942 when these P-40Es saw quite a bit of action. When Clyde Barnett got his first kill on April 25 he had only twenty-five hours flying time in the P-40. Though a Zero put three holes in his Warhawk, Barnett got a Betty, and his squadron mates managed to come through the combat with excellent results: eight Bettys and three Zeros claimed destroyed. *Clyde H. Barnett, Jr.*

Bruce Harris at the 8th Fighter Squadron alert shack, Kila Kila, New Guinea, late 1942. In many ways the grass huts were an improvement over Army-issue tents but they didn't do much to keep the bugs, snakes, and other wild things out, particularly at night.

Unfortunately, there wasn't much to do but live with them since there was no way to kill off an entire jungle of animals. The huts were not bad at beating the daytime heat. *Clyde H. Barnett, Jr.*

64

The only fighters to get airborne and do any damage during the attack on Pearl Harbor flew out of Haleiwa Strip on the north coast of Oahu. From that point on it became a dispersal point for air defense of the Hawaiian Islands. This P-40K sits in a revetment adjacent to the runway in September 1943, long after the war had gone on to other places. *Via Jack Cook*

A P-40K is pushed back into its revetment at Haleiwa Strip, Oahu, September 1943. Situated among the many trees growing next to the runway, the revetments were quite effective in camouflaging the Warhawks below. After the Pearl Harbor attack, the strip remained a gunnery training facility. *Jack Cook*

Though the P-40 served in all theaters of war except Europe, it will always be associated with China because of the Flying Tigers. Here mechanics work on a 26th Squadron, 51st Fighter Group P-40E in China. This was just about the sum total of facilities and equipment, other than an engine hoist. Discarded 55-gallon drums served as everything from jack stands to lunch tables since so many of them were brought in over the Hump. *USAF via Stan Piet*

Pet monkeys weren't much help in China, but they were a welcome relief from living and fighting on the end of a long and hard-pressed supply line. Sgt. Elmer J. Pence paints a second kill flag on this 26th Squadron, 51st Fighter Group P-40K at Kunming, late 1943, while the monkey stays busy with the artist's paint brush. The Warhawk's paint is much the worse for wear, and the black on the prop tips has been completely scoured off. *USAF*

Pilots and ground crew of the 26th Fighter Squadron seem to enjoy the pet monkey's antics as Sgt. Elmer Pence continues to paint the second kill flag on this P-40K at Kunming, China, in late 1943. The K was the heaviest of all P-40 variants at 10,000 pounds. This didn't do much for performance, in spite of an uprated Allison engine. The best performing Warhawks were the lightweight L, M, and N models, but the P-40 didn't come up to the day's standards until the XP-40Q, which was too late to see World War II service. *USAF via Stan Piet*

A Royal New Zealand Air Force Kittyhawk just airborne off Fighter Strip #1 at Bougainville, Soloman Islands, April 1944. Across the runway from this view out of Garnett Tower are Avengers, Airacobras, and Lightnings. The largest island in the Solomon chain, Bougainville was invaded by the Allies on 1 November 1943 to provide a staging base for the bombing of Rabaul. Though the last major Japanese counterattack was made in late January 1945, there were skirmishes until the end of the war. *National Archives*

A Merlin-powered P-40F on a test flight out of Buffalo in 1942. Though the first batch of aircraft had the short fuselage of the E model, a little over half the F production run incorporated a 20-inch extension as an attempt to eliminate tail flutter. The modification gave the fighter better stability, particularly on the ground during take-off and landing. Since the engine was based on the low-altitude Merlin 28 there was basically no performance improvement compared to the F's Allison-powered brothers. *NASM Arnold Collection*

A 3rd Air Commando Group P-40N flies over Alligator Point, Florida, in August 1944 as the unit trains for combat. Before heading for the Philippines, the Group would transition to the P-51 Mustang under the command of Maj. Walker "Bud" Mahurin, a famous Thunderbolt ace with the 56th Fighter Group in the European Theatre. *Jacques Young*

A P-40F undergoes field maintenance with about as many tools as could be expected under combat conditions. A liquid-cooled fighter was certainly more complex to work on than an air-cooled type. The plumbing alone for what was often referred to as the "hot water toilet," was a twisting, turning series of pipes and rubber hoses that always seemed to be in the hardest places to reach, much less get a wrench on. *USAF*

Previous page
This flight of advanced transition fighters out of Randolph Field, Texas, consists of a P-40K, a P-40R-1, and a P-40R-2. A total of 300 long fuselage P-40Fs and Ls, originally slated for Merlin engines, were modified to take Allison V-1710-81s of 1,360 horsepower and were then redesignated R-1 and R-2 respectively for use in stateside training. A quick way to spot what used to be an F or an L is to look at the wing guns. The F carried three .50s in each wing, while the L carried only two in each wing. These two Rs reflect the difference upon close examination. *USAF*

A P-40E Warhawk gets up and away on a training flight in the U.S. The pilot is wearing his overseas cap and a pair of headphones—ear and head protection was still something yet to be designed into regulation issue equipment. The flight leader's stripe would soon disappear, resurrected (unofficially) only in the last year of the war in the Pacific, particularly on P-38s. *NASM Arnold Collection via Stan Piet*

A brand new P-40N over upper New York state during a test flight out of the Curtiss factory at Buffalo. This final production version of the Warhawk was another attempt at getting as much performance as possible from the basic design. Again, saving weight was the primary thrust of the effort. Only four guns with reduced ammunition capacity were carried on these, along with aluminum oil coolers and radiators, lighter wheels, smaller fuel tank, and the same 1,200-horsepower engine fitted to the M. The result was a boost in speed to 378 miles per hour, the fastest of all models, but still far below the competition. With the P-40N-5 came a return to six guns and the improved-vision canopy that made the N so recognizable. In the end more Ns were built—5,215—than any other P-40. The last of the line, P-40N-40-CU AAF 44-47964, rolled out of Buffalo on 30 November 1944. *NASM Arnold Collection*

Gunnery training at Punta Gorda, Florida, in 1944, was centered around the P-40Ns sent brand new from the factory. With the massive output of Warhawks going on unabated, most were sent to the advanced fighter training fields in the U.S., a boon to pilots since, up to mid-1943, most of the aircraft fighter pilots learned on were worn out from hard use. Some were even war wearies returned from the active theaters. Flying a new P-40 was intoxicating; not only was the Allison and its systems virtually trouble-free, but the light controls and maneuverability of the Curtiss were an invitation to push one's limits. *John Quincy via Stan Wyglendowski*

When Army pilot Class 43-K showed up at Napier Field, Alabama, in November 1943 to go through gunnery training and fighter transition, they found these parrot-headed P-40Ns on the line. For all the shark mouths on P-40s, few could equal the color and originality of these "birds." *James G. Weir*

One of the 43-K pilots with his parrot-headed P-40N at Napier Field, Alabama, November or December 1943. The line chiefs must have had some dedicated nose artists to paint these involved and eye-catching parrots. *James G. Weir*

Jim Weir, Army pilot Class 43-K, climbs up on his parrot-headed P-40N at Napier Field, Alabama, November or December 1943. The feathers extend back to the windshield, giving the bird a real sense of flying through the air. It must have been great fun to fly one of these colorful Warhawks straight out of Advanced. *James G. Weir*

The only other pressing contract at Curtiss' Buffalo plant, in addition to the P-40, was the C-46 Commando transport, developed out of a civil airliner prototype. The aircraft was massive, clearly evident here flying with a new P-40F in early 1942. With two R-2800 engines, it was essentially a four-engine type with two oversized powerplants. This gave the C-46 a tremendous carrying capacity, more than proved later in the war when it became the single most important aircraft flying the Hump from India to China. *NASM Arnold Collection via Stan Piet*

What a surprise! When the first American fighter pilots started to wander around the airfields near Tokyo they came across an old friend. This P-40E among the ruins was one of several captured by the Japanese when they overran the Philippines and Java. Much as the Allies did during the war, enemy aircraft were restored and test flown to compare performance against line types that would be facing them. Since spares became a real issue, these fighters were often retired after short evaluation periods and then pushed aside to rot. *James G. Weir*

The unusual yellow paint job on this stateside P-40N is marred only by the camouflaged replacement cowling. Quite often the commanders of fighter transition units could paint their airplanes any way they wanted, resulting in some very interesting hot rods. *W. J. Balogh via David W. Menard*

Next page
When Fred Dyson purchased what was left of the RCAF Kittyhawk inventory on 23 October 1947, he, in a single stroke, saved much of the present P-40 population. He barged the fighters across the river from Canada to Washington state, moved them to Boeing Field, Seattle, then La Guardia, then sold them off one at a time. By 1950, one of these Kittys, AL152, was spraying crops for Washington County, Colorado, as N1207V. On 31 January 1958 it was bought by Frank Tallman and based at Palwaukee Airport, Illinois, until Tallman moved to California, where the aircraft is seen here in January 1961. *Dustin W. Carter via Dick Phillips*

Previous page
When Frank Tallman and Paul Mantz formed their movie-making and museum venture, Tallmantz Aviation/Movieland of the Air, at Orange County Airport, California, one of the finest collections of vintage aircraft was created. Here N1207V sits in front of the main office, much the worse for wear, in March 1964. By this time the original canopy had been lost in flight and a bogus N model replacement was attached, though it did not fit well at all. For the most part, Tallman flew the P-40E with no canopy at all.
Jeff Ethell

Surplus P-40s became just about everything, including gas station decorations like this 40E at Everett, Washington, 7 August 1965. This was just about the time ex-military junk was being labeled "warbirds." a term which stuck as the generic label for the movement. When someone managed to talk the owner out of his billboard, the fighter was gone through and put back in the air with Dave Tallichet's Yesterday's Air Force. It then ended up in the hands of Brian O'Farrell who sold it to Dick Hansen who now flies it as a representation of Col. Bob Scott's *Old Exterminator. Fred Johnsen*

Here's N1207V a few years later at Orange County Airport in June 1966 (when Tallmantz was in decline) with a different paint job (an RAF scheme for a few scenes in the movie *Tobruk*). The N canopy has been modified to fit the E fuselage. The Warhawk had already been mortgaged off to Rosen-Novak Auto Co., Omaha, the previous February, and on 29 May 1968 it was auctioned to A. R. Woodson for $7,000. After a long rebuild it flew in 1973 and was sold to Eric Mingledorff in 1984, then John MacGuire in July 1986. The two-seat TP-40N in the background was bought from Movieland of the Air by Kermit Weeks who will have it on airworthy display at his museum near Disney World. *Jeff Ethell*

This Fred Dyson Kitty went to several owners until being rebuilt as a corporate two-seater by Continental Steel Buildings, Burbank, California, in 1950 and 1951. Gil Macy, Montery, California, bought the aircraft in 1963 after it was damaged in an accident and flew it on the West Coast as a show plane. He leased it to 20th Century Fox as one of the airworthy P-40Es for the movie *Tora, Tora, Tora,* and the film folks managed to damage it. Tom Camp bought it in 1972 and rebuilt it (here it is with his initials on the side in November 1974) before selling it to Don Anklin in 1978, who then sold it to Flying Tiger Airlines. *Dustin W. Carter*

A boy's dream sits derelict at Pompano Beach, Florida, December 1965. Another of Fred Dyson's barged Kittyhawks, AK827 became a cloud seeder with Weather Mod Co. in Redlands, California. It was sold to Bill Ruch at Pompano in 1959 and slowly rotted away until the late Bill Ross bought the fighter in 1969. It wasn't until it was sold to Charles Nichols in 1977 that a full restoration (helped by P-40 aficionado John Paul) was started at his Yankee Air Corps, Chino, California. *David Ostrowski*

Late-March 1976: Bob Conrad straps into Ed Maloney's Planes of Fame P-40N at Indian Dunes Airstrip, California, before shooting a scene for the TV movie "Baa Baa Black Sheep," the pilot for the Black Sheep Squadron TV series very loosely based on the life of Marine Corps ace Greg "Pappy" Boyington, played by Robert Conrad. The Warhawk (AAF 42-105192, RCAF 858) is yet another of Fred Dyson's recovered fighters that ended up as a cloud seeder with Weather Modification Co. in 1956. After it crashed in 1958, Ed Maloney obtained the remains, and another derelict was made airworthy, as it remains today at Chino. *Harold R. Knowles*

When the RCAF sold their Kittyhawks in 1946, most went to Fred Dyson in Seattle. However, a few intrepid Canadians forked out their money, among them George Maude who bought P-40E AK803 (RCAF 1034) from war assets at Pat Bay Field for $50 in August 1946. He was so happy with the fighter, which had just over 500 hours total time, that he put in a bid for another at $65, just to be sure he got it. Much to his chagrin, he was outbid by $10! The Kitty, which had been stripped of its camouflage paint and polished for a 1945 war bond tour, came with ammo feed chutes and boxes, a working reflector gun sight, a zero-time Allison, and numerous spares, everything except the guns. Since that time Maude has been the sole owner of 1034, kept in a hangar near his Sidney, British Columbia, home. He runs 1034 up several times a year, operates all the systems, and keeps it in fighting trim. The aircraft's war history includes service in Alaska in the spring of 1942 with No.118 Squadron, then air defense patrols with Nos.132 and 133 Squadrons through 1945. Maude's untouched Kittyhawk is a glimpse at time standing still. *George Maude*

Index